Biblical Bedtime Stories for Kids

New Testament Amazing Moments
Pointing Your Children to God; Ages
4 - 8.

Only One Life

Only One Life

Contents

INTRODUCTION

Hey, so glad you're here. God has so much to share
• • • with us about who He is, and how much He loves us
and wants to connect with us.

This book of Biblical stories is standalone. But when com-
bined with the 'Biblical Bedtime Stories for Kids… Old Testament Amazing Moments; Pointing Your Children to God,'
you will have 365 days of either stories or prayers that will
take each family through an entire year of walking with
God.

I made a corresponding coloring book, '… New Testament
Amazing Moments; Pointing Your Children To God Coloring Book', to go with the stories from this book. The coloring book is sold separately or you can download it for free
from onlyonelifestory.com and will reinforce the teachings
to help your kids understand, visualize, and retain what is in
this book. The Old Testament Storybook also has a coloring
book to go along with it for easy visualization and hands-on
for the children. You can also buy or download it from the
same website.

This book, on its own, will take each family through 165
days of walking with God in the New Testament. The aim
is for parents to read one prayer or story per day and use
this as a basis for teaching their children about God - who

He is, what He is like, His relationship with humanity, and His moral rules for everyday living.

This book brings us the New Testament truths about Jesus and His teachings. God Almighty has a plan for us, our families, and everyone in the world from the very beginning of creation.

My thought for each family is a story or a prayer each day. **Children learn well when stories are repeated.** Because of that, I decided to write the book to alternate with either a story or a prayer, so parents can use the days of prayer to return to the story and retell it in their way or reread the story before the prayer. I wrote the prayers to encourage children to pray and praise God, show them how to express their feelings, and talk to Him as a trusted Father. The prayers are linked to the Bible stories and focus on their lessons.

In this book, we will use the most powerful name — **Jesus** — in our prayer lives. We will be thankful to God because He has said in His Word that we should be grateful in every situation. We will learn about the birth of our Lord Jesus Christ, how Satan tempted Him, and teachings from Him. We will also know how Peter prayed and raised Dorcas from death. Oh, also Paul–how he troubled the followers of Jesus Christ and eventually became one himself.

Central to the writing of this book is the belief that all humans are sinners that need a Savior and that there is only one way to our salvation–through faith in Jesus Christ, God's Son. Some people may view the stories as moral teachings, which no doubt they are. Still, the main reason I wrote this book rests on believing that both children and adults need the Savior. That is because I know, *"That if you confess with your mouth the Lord Jesus and believe in your heart that God has raised Him from the dead, you will be saved,"* Romans 10:9. Praise God! It doesn't matter if they are young. The Lord wants hearts that will believe in Him and a mouth that will confess Him.

I pray "that God will give you the spirit of wisdom and revelation in the knowledge of Him, that He will open the eyes of your understanding that you may know the hope of His calling, the riches of His glory, and the greatness of His power towards you, according to the working of His power, which He worked in Christ, when He raised Him from the dead," (Ephesians 1:17-20). In Jesus' name. Amen!

Day 1 - Zachariah Hears Some Good News

G od was all set to send His Son into the world. Nobody in Israel knew when and how this would happen. But He had promised the Israelites, His people, that He would send a special messenger first. This person would prepare the people to receive His Son when He arrived. So, they patiently waited for God to keep His promise.

This is what happened. There was a priest named Zachariah (or Zechariah or Zacharias). This priest and his wife, Elizabeth, had no children and kept praying for one. One day, while he was in the temple, an angel appeared to him suddenly. Zechariah, the priest, was afraid, but the angel told him not to be scared because God had heard his prayer. He would have a son and was to name him John.

How would you feel if you were Zachariah and heard this? He should have been pleased about this. But was he?

Day 2 - Prayer

God, I thank You so much because I know You always want to bless me.

Help me listen to You for instructions on what to do so You can bless me. I can't wait to receive another blessing from You. Thank You for Your many blessings. In Jesus' name. Amen.

Day 3 - Zachariah Does Not Believe God

An angel told Zachariah that he was going to have a son. He should have been happy because he always asked God to give him one. But maybe because he had been asking for such a long time, he did not believe what the angel told him.

So, he asked the angel, "How can this happen, for I am an old man?"

Then the angel said, "I am Gabriel who stands before God in Heaven. He sent me here to tell you this good news. But because you do not believe me, you will not be able to speak from now until the day the child is born."

Zechariah was frightened. I am sure he wished he had believed what the angel had told him. Now it was too late. We should never doubt God when He speaks His Words to us through the Bible.

Do you believe everything your parents tell you?

What is one thing the Bible says that you find hard to believe?

Day 4 - Zachariah Cannot Speak

The angel told Zachariah that he would not be able to speak until after his son was born. Zachariah must have been frightened and wondered if this was true. He soon found out because when he came out of the room in the temple, the people spoke to him, but he found out that he could not talk back to them. It happened the way the angel had said. He was now unable to speak with his mouth. He felt so ashamed. He could not wait to finish his work at the temple. As soon as he finished, he hurried back to his home in the country.

What would you do if you were Zachariah?

How would you feel?

I am sure he felt sorry for not believing God's message. Now he would be dumb for about nine months. That is a very long time.

We will find out what happens in the following story.

Day 5 - Prayer

T hank You, God, for being with me wherever I go. Dear God, help me believe Your Word when I hear or read it. Let me not doubt You because I can't see You.

My Father, I know that You are always with me, and what Your Word says is true. Give me an obedient heart that hears and quickly believes Your Word. Thank You for the Word You speak to me every day from the Bible. In Jesus' name. Amen.

Day 6 - Zachariah's Wife Expects a Baby

Zachariah hurried home from his work in the temple. He could not speak, and he had to tell his wife, Elizabeth, why. Maybe he talked to her using his hands to make signs or wrote them down. She must have been shocked to find out why he could not speak. Then one day, Elizabeth found out that she would have a baby. Now Zachariah knew that what God said was true. He was going to have the son he had always wanted. His unborn son would be a unique child, making it even more interesting. The angel had said that his unborn son, John, would make many of his people accept the Savior when He came. He was to be God's messenger to them to tell them about His Son, Jesus Christ, who would soon come to earth. That was terrific news, and God used Zachariah and Elizabeth to make this happen.

You should never forget that God uses people like you and me to do His work.

Do you know God created you with a purpose, just like John and Jesus?

Day 7 - Prayer

F ather, I am so glad that You use ordinary people like me to do Your work on earth.

I am so grateful for that. Zachariah was doing his job in the temple; his wife was doing her work at home, and when You were ready to send Your prophet, John, into the world, You chose them as his parents. Please help me keep doing the right things, and You should use me when You know I am ready to take up the task you planned for me. Thank You for having a solid plan for my life. In Jesus' name. Amen.

Day 8 - Zachariah's Son is Born

Z achariah and Elizabeth were pleased they were going to have a son. For the nine months of Elizabeth's pregnancy, Zachariah could not speak. At last, the day came when the baby was born. Everyone wanted to know what his parents were going to call him. In those days, people named their babies after their fathers or someone else from the family. Everyone expected Zachariah would do the same thing. But when the time of the baby's naming arrived, they asked his mother what the child's name was, for she was the one that could talk. She told them his name was John.

"But nobody in your whole family has that name," they said. Curious about what Zachariah might say, they answered, "Let's ask the child's father."

Zachariah could not speak still, so he asked for something to write on. Everyone waited eagerly to see what he was going to write. Would he call him John, as the angel had told him to? Zachariah knew the child was to be someone special. He also wanted to obey God. So, he wrote the word, 'JOHN', which became the baby's name.

And guess what? As soon as he did this, he could speak, just like the angel had told him.

I am sure Zechariah was glad to be able to talk again. Wouldn't you be?

If you were Zachariah, apart from just being happy to talk, what else would you have done?

Day 9 - Prayer

T hank You, God, for giving me to my parents just like You gave John to his family. Help me become the person You want me to be when I grow up. Thank You for making me special. In Jesus' name. Amen.

Day 10 - Zachariah Praises God for His Baby Boy

Zachariah named his baby boy John, just as the angel had told him to some months before. After writing that his name should be John, he could suddenly talk again. The first thing Zachariah did was praise God. He blessed God for sending him a son whom he wanted so much. He also thanked Him for making his son, John, a special messenger of Israel's soon-coming Savior. Zachariah no longer doubted God because everything the angel had told him had come true.

We should not doubt God's messages to us in the Bible.

Do you know the Bible is God's message to you?

How seriously do you take the teachings from the Bible?

Day 11 - Prayer

I praise You, my Father, for making babies like me and letting us grow up. Thank You for giving me to my parents. They take good care of me all the time, and they love me very much. It makes me so happy. Thank You for loving me, dear God. In Jesus' name. Amen.

Day 12 - An Angel Visits Mary

Before John was born, an angel visited a young woman named Mary. She was a cousin of Elizabeth, Zachariah's wife, who is the mother of John. Like John's father, God gave the angel a message for Mary. The angel told Mary that God chose her to have a special baby. The angel instructed her to give the child the name Jesus because He would save His people from their sins. He was also going to be the Son of God and the Savior promised to Israel long ago.

You see..., God had promised His people that He would send them someone to save them from their enemies. Many years had passed, and the promised Savior had not come. Now, God was about to send Him into the world.

God will always do as He promised, even if it takes a long time.

What have your parents promised you that you have been waiting to receive?

How much do you trust them to fulfill their promise to you?

Do you enjoy waiting for so long?

What can you do to calm yourself down when waiting for something?

Day 13 - Prayer

Thank You, dear God, for always keeping Your promises. Let me always remember this. You kept Your promise to Israel, and I know You will also keep Your promises to me. Please, help me keep my promises to You and my fellow human beings so that I will be like You. Thank You for making that happen. In Jesus' name. Amen.

Day 14 - Mary and the Angel

Mary felt very afraid when she saw the angel, and she was even more worried when he told her she would have a baby. But, unlike Zachariah, Mary believed what the angel said. How do I know this? I know from her reply to the angel.

After the angel gave her God's message, Mary said, "Let it happen to me as God has said."

Mary believed God right there and accepted what the angel said. We all should be more like her, quick to believe what God tells us all the time.

Do you constantly doubt what your parents tell you or always believe them?

How do you feel when you tell someone the truth and the person disbelieves you?

Day 15 - Mary Visits Elizabeth

The angel did not only tell Mary that she would have a baby boy. He also said to her that Elizabeth, her cousin, would also have a child. Mary hurried to visit her cousin in the hill country. A strange thing happened when Mary entered the house and greeted Elizabeth. The baby in Elizabeth's tummy jumped up and down. That sometimes happens to women who are expecting a baby. You might have done it, too! Ask your mother.

The two cousins were happy to see each other and shared their stories about the angel's visits and the children they were going to have. The two of them knew their babies would be extra special. They praised and thanked God for His kindness to them.

Hmm…, do you always praise God for making you unique?

What are some things you always praise God for?

Have you ever praised God for giving you free air to breathe?

Day 16 - Prayer

God, I want to thank You for my mother. She is so kind, loving, and good to me. Every day, she takes excellent care of me. She does many things to make me happy. Thank You for her, God. In Jesus' name. Amen.

Day 17 - No Room in the Inn

Mary returned home and lived with her husband, Joseph, in Nazareth. It was nearly time for her to have baby Jesus. Joseph had to go to Bethlehem for a census, so he took Mary with him. When they arrived in Bethlehem, there were lots of people. They had all come for the same reason, so the town was very crowded. Joseph tried very hard to find a room in an inn for them to stay in. He knew the baby was coming soon, but everywhere was full. There was no room in any of the inns for them.

Where were they to go? Where would baby Jesus be born?

Will you be scared if you are traveling, your parents did not find a hotel, and you all have to sleep in the car in the middle of nowhere?

Will you be scared to hear the howling of the wolves and coyotes? What about the hooting of the owls?

Day 18 - Prayer

L ord God, thank You for the birth of baby Jesus. I am sorry that no one wanted to let Mary into their house. It must have made her sad. But thank You, God, for taking care of her, Joseph, and baby Jesus that night. Help me be kind to people who need my help. Thank You very much for baby Jesus. In Jesus' name. Amen.

Day 19 - Jesus is Born

I n Bethlehem, Joseph and Mary could not find a place to stay the night, and he had to find one because Mary might soon have her baby. The only place they could find was in a stable with animals.

That night, Mary had her baby. She clothed Him in pieces of cloth and put Him in a manger to sleep. Jesus, the Son of God, was born in a stable and slept in a manger. That was something that animals eat their food from. He was not born in a castle where kings lived. He was born like a poor person, although He was God's Son. That tells us it does not matter where you are born because God is everywhere and with us always.

Have you ever asked your mom to tell you where you were born?

Were you born in a hospital, house, or barn?

Day 20 - Prayer

T hank You, God, for sending Jesus as a baby. Let me remember He is Your Christmas gift to us. I happily receive Him into my heart so that He will be with me forever. Thank You, dear Jesus, for coming into the world to be my Savior. In Jesus' name. Amen.

Day 21 - The Angels and Shepherds Celebrated Jesus' Birth

The very night Jesus was born, there were many shepherds in the field. They were watching over their sheep to keep them safe. Suddenly, an angel appeared to one group of these shepherds. The place became very bright, and the shepherds were afraid. The angel told the shepherds not to be scared. He was bringing them some very good news. Then he said to them that Jesus, the Son of God, who is the promised Savior, had just been born. He told them where He was and that they would find Him wrapped in pieces of cloth and lying in a manger.

What would you do if someone told you this?

Would you think you are dreaming?

Day 22 - Prayer

I am so glad, Father, that Jesus was born. I want to sing with the angels about Him coming to earth. I want to clap my hands, stomp my feet and shout out the wonderful good news. Hurrah! Jesus Christ, our Savior, is born! God, Thank You for sending Him to us in Jesus' name. Amen.

Day 23 - The Shepherds Visit Baby Jesus

T he angel just told the shepherds that Jesus, the Savior God had promised to Israel, was born and where to find Him. That was excellent news for them. Everyone in Israel knew of God's promise of a Savior. They had waited a very long time for it to happen. Now, at last, He was here.

So, the shepherds went and visit the baby. They wanted to see if what the angel had said was true. When they came to the manger, they found the baby and His parents. It was just like the angel told them. They were happy, and they praised God. Then they began telling everybody about this special child named Jesus. We should tell others about Jesus, God's Son and Savior of the World.

Who is the first person you will tell about Jesus, who died for the entire world?

Why is the birth of Jesus Christ good news for us?

Day 24 - Prayer

Come on, everybody, let us join with the shepherds and praise the Lord. Hallelujah! Praise the Lord! God has sent His only dear Son into the world. Let us receive Him with joy and gladness. Thank You, Lord, for your wonderful gift to us. In Jesus' name. Amen.

Day 25 - The Wise Men Follow a Star

I n a faraway country lived some Wise Men. They were constantly studying the stars in the sky. They knew stars could tell stories about what God was doing. That was one reason why God had made them. But you had to be wise to know this. The Three Wise Men spent a lot of time studying the stars to see what they meant.

When Jesus was born, they saw a very bright new star in the sky. They knew it meant a special new King was born and pointed to where He was. So, they set out from their country to find this King. The star led them, and they followed it. Do you want to know where it took them?

Have you ever looked at the stars at night?

Do you see how wonderful God is when you look at the stars?

Day 26 - Prayer

Thank You, God, for Your good works in my life. The Wise Men came looking for Jesus, dear Father, because they knew He was special. I know He is special, too, so help me find Him, just like the Wise Men. Thank You again for the newborn King. In Jesus' name. Amen.

Day 27 - The Wise Men Find Jesus

The Wise Men from a far country in the East followed a bright star they saw in the sky. They knew it was telling them about the birth of a unique King. So, they set out to find Him. They packed lots of things for their long journey. They also took some gifts for this King. They journeyed for a very long time until they came to Jerusalem. They followed the star until it stopped over a house in Bethlehem. They found Mary, Joseph, and baby Jesus when they went inside. They knew Jesus was the King the star was telling them about. They bowed down, worshipped the Savior of the World, and gave Him three gifts—gold, frankincense, and myrrh.

If we are wise, we, too, should seek Jesus today. He is no longer a child, but He is still the Savior of the World.

The Wise Men gave Jesus gifts, and we should give Him a gift, too. God only wants one gift from us—our hearts. When we give Him our hearts, He will come in and live in it, like a house. How awesome!

To give Him your heart, you need to confess with your mouth the Lord Jesus and believe in your heart that God raised Him from the dead (Romans 10:9).

Now, are you ready to give Him your heart?

Day 28 - Prayer

God, I bow down and worship You because You are the only God. There is no God who is like You in the whole wide world. I am giving myself (heart) to You as a present. Let my heart be Your dwelling place as long as I live. Please help me keep following Jesus all of my life. Thank You that You are pleased when I give myself as a gift to You. In Jesus' name. Amen.

Day 29 - Simeon Blesses Baby Jesus

M ary and Joseph always tried to obey God. He told the people of Israel to take their children to the temple to be blessed a few days after birth. So, Mary and Joseph decided to do this. While Jesus' parents went to the temple, an older man met them. He was a righteous man named Simeon. He was always praying and doing whatever God told him to do. He came into the temple where the priest was blessing Jesus.

After the priest finished blessing baby Jesus, Simeon took baby Jesus in his arms. He, too, blessed baby Jesus and said He, Jesus, was sent from God to bring God's light and glory to all people. God loves to bless little children. Even Jesus took little children in His arms and blessed them. He has a special love for children like you.

I know you have seen lots of little children. Have you ever said something good about them?

Day 30 - Prayer

Lord God, I worship Your name for who You are. Father God, I know You love me. Bless me, I pray. Mary and Joseph obeyed Your rules by taking baby Jesus to the temple to be blessed. Lord, help my parents always to follow You, too. Please enable them to do what is right. Help them take me to church to hear Your Word since I cannot go on my own. Please remind them that You have given me to them to look after. Help them know their responsibility of teaching me Your ways. Thank You, God, for I know You have answered me. In Jesus' name. Amen.

Day 31 - Anna Blesses Baby Jesus, Too

Simeon was not the only person who blessed Jesus. An older woman, Anna, was living in the temple in Jerusalem. She prayed a lot, day and night. She came into the temple while the priest was blessing Jesus. When she saw Jesus, she knew He was the promised Savior, too. She praised and thanked God for sending Him.

The birth of Jesus made angels and people praise God. That is still a wonderful thing for us to do at Christmas and year long.

Have you praised God today?

What did you praise Him for?

Day 32 - Prayer

L et us praise God today.

Let us ring the bells, "Ring-a-ling!"

Let us beat the drum, "Boom! Boom!"

Let us blow our horns, "Toot! Toot!"

Jesus is getting a special blessing today.

Let us thank the Lord God for sending His Son, Jesus, to bless us.

In Jesus' name. Amen.

Day 33 - The Wise Men Meet Herod, the King

Herod was the King of Israel. He lived in Jerusalem. Before the Wise Men found Jesus in Bethlehem, they came to Jerusalem. They had followed the star and knew that it meant that the King of the Jews was born. But they were not yet sure of the exact place.

So, in Jerusalem, they asked, "Where is He who is born King of the Jews?"

King Herod heard about this and sent them to find out where this new king was. He asked the Wise Men about Him. They told Herod about the star they had followed and how it had led them to Israel. The Wise Men had come to worship the newborn King. Herod called some Jewish writers and asked them where it was said Jesus would be born in the Bible. They told him in Bethlehem, not too far from Jerusalem. Herod then asked the Wise Men to find Jesus, come back, and tell him when they did.

He told the Wise Men, "I want to worship King Jesus, too."

Do you believe him?

Day 34 - Prayer

L ord, I want to bow down and worship the King, Jesus Christ, who is Your Son. You sent Him into the world as a gift for us. Thank You for this beautiful gift. In Jesus' name. Amen.

Day 35 - God Warns the Wise Men Not to Go Back to Herod

T he Wise Men promised to let King Herod know when they found baby Jesus. They traveled to Bethlehem, where they saw Jesus and His parents. They worshipped Him because He was the Son of God and gave Him their gifts. Then they remembered that King Herod had said he wanted to worship Jesus, too. They had promised to tell him where they found Jesus. They thought of going back to Jerusalem to let Herod know this, but an angel, in a dream, warned them not to do this. So, they left Bethlehem and returned to their country on another road.

Why did God tell the Wise Men not to return to King Herod?

Do you think God was right to tell the Wise Men not to return to Herod?

Day 36 - King Herod Tries to Kill Baby Jesus

God told the Three Wise Men not to go back to tell King Herod about finding Jesus. The king waited for them to return. When they did not come back, he realized they had tricked him. He became furious. So, he sent his soldiers to Bethlehem. He told them to kill every boy baby two years old and under. He did not want Jesus to become King of the Jews, and he tried to stay king for as long as he could. The soldiers killed many babies, and this made their families sad.

Did the soldiers kill Jesus?

How do you think the parents of the babies Herod killed felt?

Day 37 - Prayer

Thank You, God, for keeping baby Jesus safe so He could grow up to be a big man. Joseph and Mary must have been very happy they were safe from Herod's soldiers. Thank You, dear Lord, for always watching over us. In Jesus' name. Amen.

Day 38 - God Tells Joseph to Leave Bethlehem

God knows everything before it happens. That is why we must always listen to Him and obey what He says. He knew King Herod wanted to kill Jesus. So, before the king sent his soldiers to Bethlehem to kill the boy babies, the angel of God spoke to Joseph in a dream. He told him to take Jesus and His mother and run to Egypt because King Herod wanted to kill the newborn King. Joseph believed God, and so he took his family to Egypt. That was why King Herod did not kill Jesus.

It is a good thing always to obey God.

Do you always find it difficult to obey your parents?

Why?

Day 39 - Prayer

Thank You, God, for always watching over me. Thank You for the guardian angels You send to keep me safe all the time. Thank You for always taking me home safely every day I left. Thank You for being my Father in Heaven. In Jesus' name. Amen.

Day 40 - Jesus is Lost in Jerusalem

After King Herod died, God told Joseph to return to Israel. He, Mary, and Jesus went to live in Nazareth.

Every year, Jesus' family went up to the temple in Jerusalem at a particular time to worship God. When Jesus was twelve years old, Jesus and His family went up to the temple as usual. After spending a few days in Jerusalem's temple, it was time to go home.

Mary and Joseph had lots of friends with them, so they thought Jesus was in their crowd as they were returning home. But along the way, they looked for Jesus and could not find Him. They were very worried, and so they hurried back to Jerusalem. It took Jesus' parents three days to find Him.

Where did they find Jesus?

Do you always like to stay in your parents' company or your friends when you are in the park? Why?

Day 41 - Prayer

Heavenly Father and my God, I want to thank You for always being with us all the time. It must have been scary for Jesus' parents not to know where He was. But they went to the right place—Your house. That is a perfect place to be, and Jesus must have felt safe. Thank You, Lord, for taking care of us when we are lost. In Jesus' name. Amen.

Day 42 - Jesus is Found

When Jesus' parents saw Him, He was in the temple talking with some older people about the Word of God. His parents were upset because He had not come along with them. His mother asked Him why He had stayed behind because they had been worried about Him. Jesus told her He was not lost, but He was doing His Father's business. He meant His Father, God, not Joseph.

You know..., even if we have our earthly father, we still have a Father in Heaven, too. Like us, Jesus had an earthly father and a Heavenly Father. Our Heavenly Father cares so much for us. We should always talk to Him the way we speak to our earthly father.

Learning God's Word was very important to Jesus. He did not mean to be rude or hurt His parents. He was just so busy learning the Word of God that He did not remember going home. Just like Jesus, we should do everything we can to learn the Word of God because it gives life.

After they found Him, Jesus went home with His parents and was obedient to them.

What are your favorite coloring works? Are they about random kinds of stuff or the Bible?

Visit us at support@onlyonelifestory.com to receive a pdf copy you can print out to keep your kids engaged.

Day 43 - Prayer

God, I want to praise You for giving me parents that love me. Help me obey my parents, just like Jesus did. I know they love me and want the best for me. Let me not say unkind things to them or give them too much trouble. I worship Your name again. In Jesus' name. Amen.

Day 44 – John the Baptizer

While Jesus was growing into a man, His cousin, John the Baptist, was also becoming a man. But he lived in the wilderness and only ate locusts and wild honey as food.

Oooh, yummy or yucky?

Before John was born, God had told his father that John would be a messenger for Jesus. That meant that John's job was to tell people about Jesus before Jesus started His ministry. This way..., they would be ready to receive Jesus into their hearts when He comes.

It was now time for John to do this. So, one day, John began preaching about Jesus, the Savior they each needed. He told the people to get ready for Jesus because His coming was near.

We, too, must tell others about Jesus. We are now His messengers to tell everybody that Jesus is coming again and that His coming is very near. Are you ready to tell people what you know about Jesus?

What would you say about Him if I asked you to tell me about Jesus right now?

Day 45 - Prayer

Father, I praise You for promising that Jesus will come for us again. We know the coming of Jesus is near because Your Word says so. Like John, help us get ourselves ready and tell others, so they might be prepared to meet Jesus when He arrives. Again, I praise Your holy name, O God. In Jesus' name. Amen.

Day 46 - Jesus Comes to be Baptized

John kept on preaching about the coming of Jesus. He told them to prepare their hearts by turning from the wrong things they were doing. He also told them to be baptized. Many Jews came to the River Jordan, where John was preaching. Some of them turned from their sins and were baptized. Then one day, Jesus went to the river so that John could baptize Him. John was very surprised because Jesus did not have any sin. He was the Son of God, and God does not sin. John did not want to baptize Jesus, but Jesus said He had to be baptized because this was what God wanted all His followers to do. So, John baptized Jesus in the River Jordan. That day, something amazing happened.

Can you guess what happened?

Day 47 - Prayer

Thank You, Father, for sending Jesus to teach us to obey Your Word. He is Your Son, and He knew He should obey You. Teach us to be like Him—obedient to You and our earthly parents. I adore You for always being with us and helping us all the way. In Jesus' name. Amen.

Day 48 - God Shows that Jesus is Very Special

Jesus went to His cousin John so he would baptize Him. John baptized Him in the River Jordan. As Jesus emerged from the water, Heaven opened, and John saw something like a dove fly down from Heaven, and it rested on top of Jesus.

Then he heard a voice saying, "This is my beloved Son who pleases me very well."

That was God speaking. Oh wow!

Now John knows Jesus is the Son of God who came down from Heaven to earth. We must believe this, too, and welcome Him into our hearts.

What does that dove represent?

Day 49 - Prayer

D ear God in Heaven, I lift Your name on high because You made me special. That is why You sent Your only beloved Son, Jesus, to die for me. Because You did this, I know You love me very much. I want to say thank You for loving me so much. I want to spend all my life loving You back for Your goodness to me. Thank You for Your greatness. In Jesus' name. Amen.

Day 50 - Satan and Jesus

D id you know God has an enemy who hates Him? Yes, and his name is Satan. He wants to take over the world from God and rule it. He does not want to obey God, who created him, or do anything God tells him to do. He is evil. Satan tries to hurt people all the time and wants us to hurt each other. But more than anything, he wants us to disobey God. That makes him happy. So, he is always trying to make us sin. Do you want to know what he did to Jesus? He tried to make Him disobey God.

Did Satan make Jesus sin?

Day 51 - Prayer

Dear God, I am so happy whenever I remember how you smashed Satan for my sake. Please help me believe that Satan exists. I sometimes wonder if he is real because I can't see Him. But if he came and tempted Jesus, then he must be real. Please teach me how to deal with him so that I will not fall into his trap. Help me believe and I praise You, Lord, for giving me power over him. In Jesus' name. Amen.

Day 52 - Satan's First Test for Jesus

S atan wanted Jesus to disobey God, His Father, so he came to Jesus in the desert after John baptized Him. There he tempted Jesus three times to do something wrong. First, Satan told Jesus that He should turn some stones into bread if He were indeed the Son of God.

Of course, Jesus could do this and much more because He is the Son of God. Jesus was all alone, tired, and very hungry because He had not eaten for forty days and nights.

But should He?

No.

Why?

Because we must do nothing Satan tells us to do. So, Jesus did not listen to him. Jesus passed the first test.

Do you know Satan always tells the children of God to do wrong things every day?

What are some things that Satan always wants people to do?

Day 53 - Prayer

Our Father in Heaven, thank You for always being with me. Please keep me safe from the devil when he comes to tempt me to do wrong. Please assist me in being like Jesus and saying, "No!" to Satan all the time. Thank You, Lord, for giving me power over him. In Jesus' name. Amen.

Day 54 - Satan's Second Test for Jesus

J esus passed the first test from Satan. So, Satan tried to get Jesus to sin in another way. He took Jesus way up to the top of the Temple in Jerusalem. Then he told Jesus that if He were indeed the Son of God, He should throw Himself down from there. Satan even reminded Him that the Bible said God would save Him from falling if something like that happens. That was true, but only if Jesus was not falling to show off. So, Jesus told Satan, "No!" again and did not obey him.

Wow! Jesus won over Satan two times now.

Will He win the last time?

What would you have done if you were Jesus?

Day 55 - Prayer

God, You are so wonderful. You gave us the Holy Bible, filled with how we can live and know all Satan's tricks. Please assist me in understanding what the Bible says, so Satan does not trick me into doing the wrong thing. Thank You for my parents and the writer of this book, helping me understand what You want me to know from the Bible so that I can be safe. In Jesus' name. Amen.

Day 56 – Satan's Last Test for Jesus

Jesus had passed Satan's test two times. Satan certainly was not happy. He kept on losing, as Jesus would not obey him. He decided to try one last thing. He knew people liked to be rich, famous, and have lots of power. Maybe he could get Jesus to sin in one of these areas. So, he offered Jesus all the riches and control of the world. But guess what? Satan said Jesus would have to worship him before he could have those things.

Can you believe that? Was Satan the true God of the entire world? Did he make everything and give life to everyone?

No!

Jesus knew this, and so did Satan. So, Jesus said, "No!" one last time. Then Satan left Him shamefully because he knew he could not make Him disobey God.

Hurray for Jesus! He won!

We should be like Jesus, only obeying God and never Satan.

Has Satan ever tempted you before?

How did you know it was Satan?

Day 57 - Prayer

Thank You, God, that Jesus passed all the tests. Thank You, He did not let Satan win. Teach me to obey Your Word, so I, too, will pass the test when Satan tempts me to do wrong. Thank You for Your Word is powerful. In Jesus' name. Amen.

Day 58 - Jesus Chooses His Disciples

After the temptations, Jesus came back from the desert. He began to preach that the Kingdom of God was soon to come. Many people started following Him to hear what He had to say. One of the first people to follow Jesus was Andrew. He was a follower of John the Baptist. One day, he heard John say of Jesus, "Look at the Lamb of God, who takes away the world's sins!"

Andrew wanted to know what John meant by referring to Jesus as 'the Lamb of God who takes away the world's sins.' So, he began following Jesus. After a little while, he asked Jesus where He lived, and Jesus invited him to come and see. From that day, Andrew became a follower of Jesus.

Why did people follow Jesus? They wanted to know Him better and to become like Him. Jesus still invites us to follow Him today. Will you? What makes the followers of Jesus separate from the rest people?

Day 59 - Prayer

Precious Father, I want to praise You for choosing me to be Your child. I want to follow You all the days of my life to know You better. May You show me how You want me to go, so I can keep following You. Thank You for I know You have answered me. In Jesus' name. Amen.

Day 60 - More Disciples Follow Jesus

W e call people who followed Jesus when He was on earth His disciples. Today, we call them Christians. Many other people followed Jesus in His time and became His disciples. He had twelve special disciples who went with Him everywhere. After becoming a disciple, Andrew went and called his brother, Peter.

James and John were brothers, too. Jesus called them to be His disciples while they were in their father's boat on the sea, fishing. They left everything and followed Him. Jesus also called Philip, who invited Nathanael to come along because they *"have found Him of whom Moses in the law, and also the prophets, wrote—Jesus of Nazareth, the son of Joseph."* Matthew was a tax collector, and Jesus also called him to be His disciple, and he came along.

Jesus called other people, but some were too busy, some did not want to leave what they had, and some were just not interested. Those who answered His call to become disciples were the wise ones. Do you want to be a Christian, to get to know Jesus?

Remember, Jesus called all kinds of people, even children. He said, "Let the little children come to me..." (Mathew 19:14).

Then God is calling you to follow Him now. Will you be too busy or not interested in following Him? Where do you belong?

Day 61 - Prayer

F ather God, I worship You for calling me to join Your family. It is so good to have You as my Father in Heaven. Let me tell others how good this is, so they will want to join Your family, too. I cannot stop telling You, "Thank You" for making me part of Your family. In Jesus' name. Amen.

Day 62 - Jesus' First Miracle

One day, Jesus and His disciples were invited to a wedding in Cana of Galilee. Jesus' mother, Mary, was also there. Everyone enjoyed themselves, eating and drinking merrily.

Then, Jesus' mother came to Him and said, "The wine is finished."

That was not a very good thing for the new husband and wife. People would say bad things about them when they found out there was no more wine. Mary wanted to help them. That was why she came to Jesus. She knew He could work miracles. Jesus decided to help them. So, He told the servants to fill six huge clay jars with water. Then He told them to draw some out of the jars and give them to the master of the feast. When the servants took what they drew out of the jars to the master of the feast, the water had turned into wine. The servants told everyone about it, which helped many people to believe that Jesus was indeed the Son of God.

That was the first miracle of Jesus.

Hallelujah!

Have you ever been to a wedding before?

Did you eat? What kind of food did you eat?

What kind of drink did you drink?

Day 63 - Prayer

My Most High God, thank You for Your Son, Jesus. He was so kind and good to these people. I know He wants to be like that to me, too. Let me always remember to come to You when I have a problem and to obey what You tell me to do. Thank You because You said You would answer me if only I would dare to ask You anything in the name of Jesus. I know; I have to ask according to Your Word, though. Thank You, my Promise Keeper. In your name, I pray. Amen.

Day 64 – Nicodemus Talks to Jesus

J esus went around Judea and other places, telling people about the Kingdom of God and how to get into it. But not everyone understood what He was saying. Some of them who did not understand wanted to know more. One such man was Nicodemus. He was a ruler among the Jews. He taught them the Word of God. Even so, he did not understand what Jesus was talking about. So, he went and ask Him on his own.

He came to Jesus one night and talked with Him. Jesus told him many things about God's Kingdom and how to enter it. Nicodemus learned a lot from Jesus about the Kingdom that night. When we don't understand something, it is always a good thing for us to ask.

Jesus always preached about the Kingdom of God. What is the Kingdom of God, anyway?

What do you have to do to enter the Kingdom of God?

Day 65 - Prayer

Dear God, thank You for being so friendly to people. Lord, sometimes I want to talk to Jesus like Nicodemus did. I have so many questions I want to ask. Teach me to read Your Words every day so that I can find some answers. Thank You for helping me with Your Word. In Jesus' name. Amen.

Day 66 - Be Kind to One Another

One Sabbath day, Jesus was in a synagogue teaching the people. Sabbath was the day God told the Jews to rest and not work. Some of the Pharisees, the Jewish holy men, were there. There was also a man with a withered hand. They watched Jesus closely to see if Jesus was going to heal the man on the Sabbath day. Jesus then asked them if it was good to do good on the Sabbath day. He wanted to know if they would say He broke God's rule if He helped someone who was sick on a Sabbath day.

Jesus said, "Is it right to take your sheep out of a hole it fell on the Sabbath day?"

They all knew the sheep would die if no one took them out. So, the answer was yes. To show them that this was true, Jesus healed the withered hand of the man. No one could say anything. They now knew that saving someone's life or doing good to someone on the Sabbath day was not wrong.

It is never wrong to do something good for someone.

Have you done something good for someone today?

What are some of the good things you do for people?

Day 67 - Prayer

God, I bless Your name for always giving us good gifts. Sometimes, though, we don't want something good to be done for others because we are just mean and selfish like these people. Let me be happy when You do good things for others. Lord, I thank You because Your bank of good stuff for us does not run out. In Jesus' name. Amen.

Day 68 – Jesus Helps a Woman from Samaria

J esus and His disciples were going to Jerusalem. To get there, Jesus went by the town of Samaria even when He knew that the Samaritans and the Jews were enemies. They hardly even talked to each other. Jesus and His disciples were all hungry and thirsty. So He sent them to buy food while He sat alone by the well and waited for them.

As He sat there, a woman from Samaria came to the well to get water, and Jesus asked her for some water to drink. She was surprised that Jesus spoke to her because she was a Samaritan, and the Jews did not talk to them. But Jesus spoke kindly to her and told her He was the promised Savior. She believed Him and ran to tell others about the good news. The other Samaritans quickly came, and Jesus taught them. They were so happy to have met Jesus, the promised Savior.

We must always be kind to others and share the good news about Jesus with people.

Will you be able to talk to someone who hates you as Jesus did?

What will you do if you talk to the person and he refuses to answer or speak to you roughly?

Day 69 - Prayer

F ather, thank you for giving me the power to talk to people about You and Your wonders. Please help me tell others about You all the time. Sometimes, I want to, but the words won't come, or I am afraid. Let me remember You are always with me and that You have not given me the spirit of fear, but of power, love, and a sound mind. Thank You, for Your Word is powerful. In Jesus' name. Amen.

Day 70 - Jesus Heals a Nobleman's Son

One of the things Jesus did when He was on earth was miracles and healing the sick. This way, people knew He was the Son of God. Many people believed in God when they saw the miracles Jesus did, and Jesus obeyed His Father and worked many mighty works.

This was one of them. A nobleman had a son who was very sick. He came and asked Jesus to follow him home so He could heal his son, but Jesus worked a miracle instead. He did not go to the nobleman's house, and he just told him that his son would be better when he arrived home. The nobleman did not doubt what Jesus said, and he believed Jesus. He returned home to discover that his child had recovered from his illness. That is the power of God at work.

Hallelujah!

When you are sick, what do you do?

Have you ever asked pain to get out of your body in the name of Jesus?

Day 71 - Prayer

God, You are so good. Your Son, Jesus Christ, healed people—the rich, poor, soldiers, women, and children from their diseases. That shows that You and Jesus love all of us, which makes me feel so good. I am happy You are my God and Father. Thank You again for Your goodness in my life. In Jesus' name. Amen.

Day 72 - The Healing of the Man Beside the Pool

Here is another healing miracle that Jesus did. There was a man who had been sick for thirty-eight years. That's a long, long time. He could not walk, and he waited by the pool at Bethesda every day, hoping to get better. Many other sick people were there, too.

You see..., often, an angel came down and stirred up the water in the pool. The first sick person who entered the pool after the angel stirred the water was healed! For this poor man, getting into the pool first was impossible because someone always stepped in before him.

One day, Jesus came by. Out of all the sick people, He spoke to this man and asked him if he wanted to get better. The man complained instead of saying, 'Yes.' Jesus didn't mind his complaining. He told the man to take up his bed and walk. Immediately, the man took up his bed and walked. He was healed by believing and obeying Jesus.

That was good news for the man because he stood up and took his bed the moment Jesus told him. No more complaining, hey?

Come to think of it, why do people complain?

What is the difference between complaining and making a point?

Day 73 - Prayer

My Father in Heaven, thank You so much for all the many blessings You have for me. Let me learn to obey You so I can receive the blessings You have stored up for me. I know, for sure, that it must have been a very happy day for the sick man. I am so glad when You do great things for others and me. Dear Lord, there are lots of children in the hospital. Some are even in the Intensive Care Unit (ICU) right now. Please help them, just like You helped the man at the pool. Thank You for always being so helpful. In Jesus' name. Amen.

Day 74 - The Story of the Lost Sheep

J esus liked to tell stories to teach the people about God and His Kingdom. Once, He told them the story of the lost sheep. A man had one hundred sheep.

"Baa! Baa! Baa!" They were everywhere.

The shepherd took very good care of his sheep. He led them out to the green grass every day so they could eat. He watched over them while they ate so no animal could harm them. He brought them back home in the evenings and locked them into their pen. This way, he kept them safe. He counted them when he took them out and when he brought them back home. But one day, he counted them in the evening, and one was missing. He was very worried about this one sheep. So, he left the ninety-nine and looked for the one lost sheep. He never came back until he found that little sheep. He was so excited to have found the one sheep that he called his friends together to tell them the good news.

What do you think about the shepherd? Was he greedy or caring? Why was he greedy or caring?

Day 75 - Prayer

I want to bless Your name, dear Lord, for always guiding us. Sometimes, God, I feel like a little lamb that runs away and does naughty things. Father God, Jesus is the Good Shepherd. Please help me be a good little lamb and obey everything He tells me to do. Thank You, Lord, for always keeping an eye out for me and bringing me back whenever I get away. In Jesus' name. Amen.

Day 76 – The Son Who Went Away

Jesus told a story about a man who had two sons. They lived with him and worked on his farm.

One day, the younger son said to his father, "Please, give me the money that is mine."

The father gave him the money that belonged to him. A few days later, the younger son packed his things and went away to a distant place to live. There, he partied, had fun, and spent all of his money. When he finished using all his money, his friends left him. He had nowhere to go and no food to eat. He had to find a job. The son ended up working on a pig farm. Sometimes, he was so hungry that he ate some of the pigs' food for dinner.

Yuck!

Life was very hard. He was unhappy, so he came to his senses and decided that he did not want to live like this. Then he remembered his father's house, where there was always food and many servants. Maybe he should return there. But what would his father say and do to him? Would he chase him away or take him back?

What do you do when you offend your parents or anyone?

What does it takes to say, "I'm sorry"?

Day 77 - The Boy Returns to His Home

T he younger son kept wondering what his father would do to him as he traveled back home. He had left home a long time ago, and now he was coming back. But things were different now. He had gone with lots of money, and now he had none. He'd left with many fancy clothes; now, they were old, dirty, and torn up. Then, he had lots of food to eat, but now he was starving. He had spent all his money doing foolish things. He had been a very naughty boy, and now he felt very sorry for all the bad things he had done.

As he came closer to their house, he saw his father's house way down the road. Maybe he could turn back, or he should try to sneak inside without his father knowing right away. Yes, that would be a good thing for him to do. But as he came nearer, he saw someone running down the road towards him.

Oh no! It was his father!

What was he going to do now?

If you were this young man, what would you have done?

Day 78 - Prayer

I bless You, dear Lord, for Your mercies are new every morning. God, when I do wrong things and go away from You, please don't let me stay away forever. Let me feel sorry and come back to You because You are a good Father. Thank You for constantly receiving me whenever I come back. In Jesus' name. Amen.

Day 79 - The Kind Father

The son stood up and watched his father running down the road towards him. He was too far away to see if his father was happy or mad. As his father came closer, the son looked at his face, and it was filled with joy as he rushed up to him, then his father hugged him tightly.

"Oh, my son! I'm so glad to see you!"

The younger son could not believe what he was hearing. His father was happy to have him back.

"Father, I am sorry for what I did," he said, sobbing. "I am not fit to be called your son. Let me be just a servant in your house."

But his father was not listening to him. He was calling his servants. "Bring the best robe, shoes, and my special ring for my son. Hurry and kill the best cow so we can have a feast."

The son could not believe the kindness of his father. He had forgiven him for all the wrong things he had done. It was the most beautiful thing that had ever happened to him.

Just like this father, God is ready to forgive us, too, for any wrong things we have done once we are truly sorry.

Was it right for the father to forgive his son after all he had done?

What does it mean to forgive someone?

Day 80 - Prayer

Thank You, Father God, for always being so forgiving. Help me remember that You always love me, no matter what I do. I can always come back to You and ask for Your forgiveness. Your arms, O Lord, are always wide open to receive and forgive me. That is wonderful to know. You are so awesome, God, and I love you so much! In Jesus' name. Amen.

Day 81 - The Older Brother

The father was thrilled that his long-lost son had found his way home. He had a party for him. The food was cooking; the music was playing, and there was a lot of laughing and talking.

Now, this father also had an older son. He was well behaved and had stayed at home with his father. Like the younger son, he had never taken his things and left home. He was at work in the fields when his brother came back. As this older brother came near the house, he heard the music.

"What's going on?' he asked one of the servants.

"Oh, your brother has returned home, and your father is happy. He's having a party for him."

 "A party, you say?' he asked, to make sure he was getting it right.

"Yes," replied the servant. "Isn't it great?"

What do you think the older brother is going to say to this?

Face it, if you were him, what would you have done?

Day 82 - Prayer

G od, I want to thank You for Your Word that says the angels in Heaven are happy when we are born into Your family. They are so glad for even one person that receives you. They rejoice, sing, and shout, "Hallelujah, to the Lord! Someone has come home!" Thank You, Lord God, for loving us so much that You hold a party in Heaven for a saved soul. In Jesus' name. Amen.

Day 83 - The Angry Brother

The older brother could not believe what he was hearing. His younger brother had run off and did not tell them where he was. He had left him to do all the hard work, and now he has come back, and his father is giving him a party. Did their father forget that he took all the money and has come back home with none of it? His father must be crazy to be throwing a party for one who had acted up. Well, he will not attend the party. He was too angry and upset. He decided to stay outside until it was over. That was just not right. And he was going to let his father know how he felt about it.

What do you think happened after this?

What do you do when things don't go as planned?

Day 84 - Prayer

Father, thank You because You are always blessing people. Let me not be angry when You do good things for others. We all belong to You, and everything is Yours to give to whomever You wish. Let me be happy that You bless others, too. Thank You for Your many blessings. In Jesus' name. Amen.

Day 85 - What About Me?

The older brother was very angry with his father for throwing a party for his younger brother. So, he decided not to go to the party. He stayed outside, and his father came looking for him.

"Why aren't you inside at the party?" he asked.

"Because I don't think you are fair to me?" the older son said.

"What do you mean?" his father asked.

"Imagine, I have been here with you all the time. I did all the work while my brother was away, and you have never had a party for me."

"Oh, my son," his father said. "Don't you know that all I have is yours, and if you wanted a party, all you had to do was ask?"

"But...but...this son of yours wasted all that money, and you still welcome him back?" he said.

"Yes, son...he says he is sorry, and I have forgiven him...this is what fathers do because they love their children."

"I am a forgiving father...my love will not let me do anything else... and you must learn to forgive him, too."

The father was right. God tells us that we must always forgive those who have done wrong.

Has anyone done wrong to you?

Were you able to forgive the person?

Day 86 - Prayer

God, I bless Your name for Your kindness. Help me not to be like this older brother. He did not want to forgive his younger brother. Let me obey Your Word, which says we are to forgive each other and be happy when God forgives others, no matter how naughty they have been. Thank You for always forgiving us. In Jesus' name. Amen.

Day 87 – A Roman Soldier Believes in Jesus

J esus was busy preaching and teaching the people. They came from all over to hear this new teacher. When he went to a town named Capernaum, a Roman soldier came to Him. Now the Romans were the rulers of the Jews, and they were not friends. Sometimes, the soldiers treated the Jews badly and even killed them. While He was in the town, the soldier came to Him. He asked Jesus to heal his servant, who was very sick.

Jesus said to the Roman soldier, "I will come to your house and heal him."

But the soldier said, "No, You don't have to come. You can just speak from here, and my servant will be healed."

Jesus was amazed at the man for believing so much in Him. So, He told him that he would find his servant well when he got back home.

It happened just as Jesus said, and the soldier was pleased.

What made you think the Roman soldier was able to believe so much in the Word that Jesus would speak?

Day 88 - Prayer

Dear God, thank You for You are love. Help me have the kind of faith that believes what You say right away. Your Word says if we do not have faith, we cannot please You. I want to please You all the time, so help me always believe and do what You tell me. Thank You because You have done everything from the very beginning. In Jesus' name. Amen.

Day 89 - Jesus Calms the Sea

One beautiful day, Jesus and His disciples were crossing over a sea on a ship. He was tired from talking to people all day. He fell asleep at the back of the boat. Suddenly, the winds started to blow, and a big storm came up. It rocked the ship up and down. The disciples were very afraid.

"We're all going to drown!" they cried.

Then one of them said, "But Jesus is on the ship. Let's ask Him to help us."

Quickly, they found Jesus and woke Him up.

"Master," they said. "Help us, or we're all going to die."

Very calmly, Jesus stood up and said to the sea, "Peace, be still."

At that moment, the winds stopped, and the waves calmed down. Jesus even had power over the sea! His disciples were amazed.

Do you know you have power in the words you speak?

Oh, yes! That is why you should mind what you say every time.

Day 90 - Prayer

I love You, Lord, because You are always with us. When I am afraid, God, please let me trust You. I believe I can face anything so long as You are with me. Let me remember Your promise never to leave me by myself or let me face any trouble alone. Remind me to always call upon You whenever I am afraid. Thank You, Lord, because You said You would answer us whenever we call on You. In Jesus' name. Amen.

Day 91 - The Wise Man and the Foolish Man

Jesus told a story about two men. One of them was wise, and the other was foolish. Both men were building their houses. The wise man took a lot of time making his house. He wanted it to last. So, he dug deep into the rock to ensure it would not fall easily. The foolish man was in a hurry. He did not want to dig deep. That took too much time. So, he built his house on the sand.

The foolish man finished his house long before the wise man could finish his house. He might have been lying down and wondering what the wise man was doing for so long!

Then the heavy winds and rains came and beat upon the two houses. What do you think happened? Right. The wise man's house did not fall, but the foolish man's house crashed. So be smart and make sure you build your life on Jesus, the Solid Rock, and the Chief Corner Stone.

Have you ever built a sandcastle on the beach before?

Have you built a tent either during camping or make-believe?

What did you use to build them?

Did they stand when the wind blew?

Day 92 - Prayer

Thank You because You are a gracious God. My Father, I always want to be wise and do things the way You say I should. Let me not be foolish like this man and lose everything because I did not build my life on Your Word. I want my house to be standing after the storms of life are over. Thank You for making me wise. In Jesus' name. Amen.

Day 93 - The Many Seeds

J esus again told a story about a farmer who went out into the field to sow seeds. He took a handful out of the bag and scattered them about. Some seeds fell by the wayside. The hungry birds quickly came and ate them up. That was the end of those seeds. They did not have time to grow. The next set of seeds fell on stones and not into the ground. A bit of soil was there, so they grew up quickly. But the sun's heat dried them up, and they died. The third set of seeds fell among thorns and weeds. They grew for a while. But then, many thorns and weeds grew up around them and choked them. So, they, too, died. Oh-oh! Poor farmer, he only has one set of seeds left now. What is going to happen to those seeds? The last set of seeds fell upon the farmer's good ground prepared for them. And guess what? They grew and bore many other seeds.

The wayside, stones, thorns/weeds, and finally, the good ground, represent the different hearts of people. Which ground do you think Jesus would want your heart to be like? Why did you choose your answer?

Day 94 - Prayer

I thank You, Lord, for always being so good. Lord God, give me a heart like the good ground, so my life will show how good You are. Let me not be in too much of a hurry to grow or be so busy doing what I want that I have no time to serve You. Help me make obeying Your Word the most important thing in my life. Thank You for everything You have done for me. In Jesus' name. Amen.

Day 95 – The Wheat and the Tares

J esus talked a lot about farming in His stories. He said God's Kingdom is like a farmer sowing seeds in his field. These are seeds that will bear other seeds, good for eating. But then, along comes an evil man who planted weeds in his field. He does this at night when no one is around. So, the farmer does not know that he is doing this. The wheat and the weeds grew together. Only when the seeds were growing and bearing fruit did the servants see the weeds. They hurried to the farmer and asked him if they should pull out the weeds now. But the farmer said no. They were to leave them to grow together until harvest time. Then he would separate the wheat from the weeds. The wheat he would use to make bread. Then, he would burn up the weeds because they were not good.

Have you ever seen a wheat farm before? If you have, what do they look when they are small and what do they look like when it is time for harvest?

Will you be wheat or weed seed? How?

Day 96 - Prayer

L ord, thank You for the power of choice You have given us—we can decide what we want to do. Dear Lord, I have decided to be like the wheat. I don't want to be a weed that looks good but is not. You know everything about us, God, for we cannot hide from You. When Jesus comes back to earth, everybody will know who was good and who was not. I want to be good right now and until You come. Please help me accomplish what I have decided on—being good all the time. Thank You for answering my prayers. In Jesus' name. Amen.

Day 97 - When Small Is Great

J esus liked to talk about seeds. They helped His listeners understand how the Kingdom of God worked. He told them about a mustard seed. It was one of the smallest seeds the people knew. Jesus said it was a very tiny seed, but it became a massive plant when it grew up. It was so big that birds of the air came and perched in it.

Think of that—something small can grow enormous for others to use. How about you? You are small, but God can use you in a big way in people's lives around you.

Are you willing to be used by God?

Name three ways you think God can use you to help others.

Day 98 - Prayer

God, I worship You because I am not too small to do something for You. Please tell me what You want me to do, and I will do it. I know I will not always be small. One day, I will grow up big. Then, I can do lots more things for You. Thank You for that. In Jesus' name. Amen.

Day 99 - Jesus Not Accepted in His Hometown

Jesus was going around everywhere preaching, teaching, and healing people. Large crowds followed Him wherever He went. Then one day, He came back to Nazareth, where He grew up. Do you think the people were happy to see Him?

They were not.

They started to talk about how they knew Him from when He was a child. His brothers and sisters had grown up with them. His father, Joseph, was only a carpenter, and they knew His mother, Mary, very well. So, they decided Jesus was pretending to be somebody important when He wasn't.

However, they were wrong because Jesus was and is the Son of God and the Savior of the World. We all need Him because He is the most important person who has ever lived.

Never forget this!

Have you ever been rejected by a group of friends before?

If you have, how did you feel?

If you haven't, would you see it kind enough to pray for some people who want others to accept them, but they are not because maybe they are sick or something else?

Day 100 - Prayer

F ather God, I praise You for being very good to me. My God, I want You to know that Jesus is always welcome where I am. I think He is so awesome and special. He left the beautiful Heaven and came to earth to live as a man. He went about teaching and doing good. That's real love! He did nothing wrong, and He paid the price for our sins by dying on the cross. You know what? Dear Lord, every time I think about Jesus leaving Heaven and everything He suffered for my sake, I always say, "Wow!" Thank You, Jesus, for being You. In Jesus' name. Amen.

Day 101 - The Little Boy's Lunch

O ne day, Jesus was preaching to many people in a desert place. They had been listening to Him all day. They had taken no food with them, and now they were all hungry. Jesus' disciples came and told Him to send the people away to get their food.

But Jesus said, "They do not have to go away. Give them something to eat."

The disciples looked at Him strangely and said, "All we have is a little boy's five loaves and two fishes. That was his lunch," they concluded.

Jesus said to His disciples, "Bring them to me."

He told His disciples to make the people sit down on the grass. Then He prayed and broke the five loaves and two fishes and gave them to His disciples to give to the people. They could not believe it. Every time they broke the bread and the fishes, there was always more left. Five thousand men, many women, and children ate from the fishes and the loaves that day.

That was a miracle.

Jesus is a great miracle worker.

What is a miracle? Are miracles still happening or not?

Day 102 - Prayer

God, thank You for always giving to people in need. Lord, this little boy was very kind. I want to be like Him and not be selfish. I want to give all I have to Jesus so He can use it to help others. Help me look around for people who need help and do what I can to help them—maybe give a drink of water or say sorry to someone crying. Thank You because I know You will help me do this. In Jesus' name. Amen.

Day 103 – Peter Walks on Water

Peter and some of Jesus' disciples were in a boat on the sea. The winds were blowing strongly, and the waves were very high. The disciples were terrified, especially since Jesus was not with them. Then suddenly, they saw someone coming toward them. It must be a ghost because people can't walk on water. Now they were terrified. Then, as the person came nearer, they realized it was Jesus. But they were still not sure.

So, Peter said, "Jesus, if that is You, let me come to You on the water."

Jesus told him, "Come."

Then Peter stepped out of the boat. And guess what? He walked on top of the water. Peter could not believe it! He was doing the impossible. Yes, with Jesus' help, we can do the impossible, too.

How would you feel if you saw someone walking on top of the water on the beach?

Day 104 - Prayer

Miracle Worker, I bow before You today. God, this was a very wondrous miracle. I want to walk on water, too. That must be very cool! That tells me again that we can do all things with Your help. For now, while I might not walk on water, please help me trust You to do whatever You tell me. I now know that whatever You ask us to do, we can do it with Your help. Thank You because You said we should ask, and whatever we ask in the name of Jesus, we will receive it. In Jesus' name. Amen.

Day 105 – The Forgiving Master

O nce again, Jesus told a story. He said there was a servant of a rich man. He borrowed lots of money from his master, and the servant could not pay it back. His master decided to sell him and his family to pay for the money he owed, but the servant fell at the feet of his master and begged him to have mercy on him. The master forgave him. The servant did not have to pay back the money, and his master did not sell him and his family.

Now, this same servant had a friend who had borrowed money from him, and the friend could not pay him back.

What do you think this servant did to his friend?

Day 106 - Prayer

Thank You, our Most High God, for being so kind to forgive us when we do wrong. Thank You because You have forgiven me for all my sins. Thank You for preparing a place in Heaven where I will live with You forever one day. I bless Your name, O God. In Jesus' name. Amen.

Day 107 – The Unforgiving Servant

D o you remember the servant whose master had for-given the money he owed him? He was very, very glad about it. This same man had a friend who owed him lesser money and could not pay him back. He became very upset with his friend and threw him into prison. When the other servants heard about it, they thought it was a terrible thing to do. They knew how their master had forgiven him for his debt. So why could he not do the same for his friend? These servants went and told their master what this servant had done. His master was upset and threw the unforgiving servant into prison. He was happy to be forgiven for the money he owed, but he did not want to forgive his friend.

We must always learn to treat others how we want them to treat us.

Come to think of it, is it easy to forgive someone?

Whatever your answer is, you can do everything through Christ that gives you strength.

Day 108 - Prayer

Dear God in Heaven, thank You so much for forgiving me of my sins even before I was born. I know I do not always treat others how I want them to treat me, and I think more about what I want and how I will receive it. Let me remember that You know my thoughts, whether good or bad. Please help me put myself in the place of others when I am talking or playing with them. Thank You for being so kind to us. In Jesus' name. Amen.

Day 109 – Who Is My Neighbor?

"Love your neighbor as yourself," says the Bible.

A particular lawyer heard this and wanted Jesus to tell him who was the neighbor he was supposed to love. Most people think your neighbor is someone who lives near you. Jesus told the lawyer this story to show him and us who our neighbor is.

One day, a Jew was going from Jerusalem to Jericho. Some thieves attacked and robbed him. They wounded him and left him to die. A certain priest (a Jew) came by, and when he saw the wounded man, he walked to the other side of the road and went away. A Levite (also a Jew) came along. He, too, looked at the bleeding man and did the same thing as the priest. Poor man, nobody wanted to help him. He was certainly going to die. Then a Samaritan came along. When he saw the man, he looked at him. He saw he was hurt.

And what do you think he did?

Day 110 - Prayer

My Father and God, thank You for loving me so much, even if I don't realize it. You said we are to love our neighbor as we love ourselves. Sometimes, I, too, wonder who my neighbor is. I can't wait to hear the following story to find out. I am so excited! Thank You, Jesus, for being my best storyteller. In Jesus' name. Amen.

Day 111 - The Good Neighbor

The man from Samaria looked at the man lying in the pool of blood at the side of the road. He was left there, hurt and bleeding, by the robbers. What was the Samaritan going to do? Would he walk away like the other two men? He felt sorry for the man, so he stopped and helped him. He did not know him, but this did not matter. He saw he needed help. So, he tied up his cuts after pouring oil and wine on them. Then the Samaritan traveler put the injured man on his donkey and took him to an inn. There, he paid the innkeeper to take care of him. He also promised to stop by and check on him the next time he came by.

Which of the three individuals do you think was a good neighbor to this man? If your answer is the Samaritan, then you are right. The good neighbor was the Samaritan, who stopped to help the wounded man. Now, you know our neighbor is anyone needing our help. We do not need to know them, and they don't have to be our friends.

We are here to help each other.

Have you helped someone you didn't know before?

What kind of expression did you see on their face?

Day 112 - Prayer

F ather God, thank You for helping me know who my neighbor is. I want to be a good neighbor. Let me stop and help other children at my school, even if they are not my friends or I don't know them. I know now that my neighbor does not have to live next to me or be my friend. Help me be kinder and more caring to those who need help. Thank You, O God, for giving us, good neighbors. In Jesus' name. Amen.

Day 113 - Zacchaeus wants to See Jesus

Z acchaeus was a very short man. He was so short that other people looked like giants to him. However, he was an important man and very rich. One day, Zacchaeus heard Jesus was coming to his town for a visit. He had heard about all the wonderful things Jesus was doing. Zacchaeus wanted to see Him. But wherever Jesus went, large crowds followed Him. Zacchaeus knew he would not stand a chance of seeing Jesus in the crowd because he was so short. Aha! He was going to climb up in a tree right where Jesus was going to pass. This way, he could look down and see Him.

Do you think Zacchaeus' plan worked?

Day 114 - Prayer

L ord God, I worship You because You know our heart, and You will always show yourself to anyone that wants to see You. Sometimes, God, I feel like Zacchaeus. I don't fit in with the others, and they tease me. Help me not let that keep me from coming to You because You know all about me and love me the way I am. I want to see You one day, so I will keep following You. Thank You because I know You will always show Yourself to me even when problems and difficulties are trying to keep me from seeing You. In Jesus' name. Amen.

Day 115 - Zacchaeus Meets Jesus Part 1

Z acchaeus wanted to see Jesus very much. But he was very short. So, he looked for a tree that hung right over the road where Jesus was going to walk. As Jesus came along the road, He saw the crowds and heard the loud chatter of the people. Long before He and the crowds came, Zacchaeus climbed up into the sycamore tree and hid. Everyone was excited. Zacchaeus could hardly wait as Jesus got closer to the tree. He would be right over Jesus' head, and no one would see him. He watched as Jesus came along the road. Then, as He came under the sycamore tree, He stopped right below Zacchaeus. Zacchaeus watched to see what He was going to do. Then Jesus looked up into the tree, exactly where Zacchaeus was hiding.

He said, "Zacchaeus, hurry and come down. For today, I must go with you to your house."

How do you think Zacchaeus felt? And what did he do?

Day 116 - Zacchaeus Meets Jesus Part 2

J esus came and stood right under the tree where Zacchaeus was hiding. Then He called Zacchaeus by his name and told him to come down from the tree. How did Jesus know Zacchaeus was up in the tree?

Zacchaeus was amazed that Jesus knew his name and where he was hiding. Jesus knew because He is the Son of God, and like His Father, God, He knows everything. Zacchaeus was so happy to have Jesus come to his house, which was much better than just seeing Him. He hurried down the tree and took Jesus home with him.

Would you be happy if Jesus came to your house today?

What would you show and tell Him?

Day 117 - Prayer

Father God, thank You for always showing Yourself to us. God, Jesus knew all about Zacchaeus, and He even knew his name and where he was hiding in the tree. Wow! I am glad that You know all about me and want me to be a part of Your family, which makes me so happy. Thank You, my Father, for inviting me into Your family. In Jesus' name. Amen.

Day 118 – Jesus Goes Home with Zacchaeus

Of course, Zacchaeus must have given Jesus something to eat, and since other people came along, they must have had some food.

As Jesus talked with Zacchaeus, the little man said, "Jesus, I am going to give half of all I own to the poor."

Jesus must have been very excited to hear this. I am sure the poor people were glad to hear this, too, for Zacchaeus was a wealthy man.

Then Zacchaeus said, "And all those people I have cheated to become rich, I will give them back four times what I took from them."

Now Zacchaeus must have sounded like a madman to be doing these things.

Why would he want to do this?

When Jesus comes to visit us, we want to be kind and good, just like Him. That was what happened with Zacchaeus. The joy of seeing Jesus, knowing that Jesus knew him, and accepted him, even if he was a fraud, made him want to do good things to show Jesus that he was grateful.

What good deed do you want to accomplish today for Jesus?

Day 119 - Prayer

L ord Jesus, thank You so much for being a friend of sinners. Father God, I would be so happy if Jesus came to my house today because there are many things I want to tell, show, and ask Him. But since I can't see You with my physical eyes but see You with my heart, I will keep talking to You when I pray. Thank You for making a way for me to speak to You whenever I want. In Jesus' name. Amen.

Day 120 - The Rich Young Ruler

O nce there was a wealthy young man. He went to the temple to pray. He read his Bible, and he tried to be kind to everyone. One day, he came to hear Jesus teach.

He asked Jesus, "What must I do to live forever?"

Jesus told him he had to keep all of God's commandments. The young man told Jesus that he had kept them all since childhood, and that sounded very good.

Then Jesus told him, "Okay, then sell everything you have, then come and follow Me."

Did the young man do this?

No, because he was wealthy and loved his money more than God. We must be cautious so that loving money or anything else does not keep us from following or obeying God.

What is your best game?

Do you get angry when your parents ask you to stop playing your game so you can do your chores?

Day 121 - Prayer

Thank You, Lord, for Your teachings are true. God, help me not love money or anything else better than You. Jesus said it is tough for a rich man to enter God's Kingdom, and it is true. When we have lots of things, we might forget about You and trust in the things we have instead. Thank You for always being there to help us. In Jesus' name. Amen.

Day 122 - The Foolish Rich Man

T here was once a farmer who had lots of lands. He planted much grain, and the ground bore a lot of wheat. That made him very happy.

He said to himself, 'What will I do with all this wheat?'

Then he had an excellent idea. He would pull down all his old barns and build bigger ones. This way, he could store up all his wheat. He would have a lot of food to enjoy for a very long time. He was only thinking about himself, and he did not think of giving any to the poor people, who had no farms or wheat. He didn't even recognize God, who had made him wealthy.

That night, God said to him, "You are foolish because tonight you will die and who will get all your wheat?"

It must have shocked the man to hear this. God wanted him to know that it was not good to think only of yourself and not of others. When God blesses you with a lot, you are to give some to those who do not have as much as you.

Have you ever given something to someone who has not?

How did you feel doing that good deed?

Day 123 - Prayer

Father God, I praise You, for You are the giver of life. Help me be kind with the things You have given me. You like it when we share what we have with others, because this is what You have done for us. You share Your love and Your goodness with us every day. You give us rain, sunshine, food, and many other things. But more than anything else, you gave Your Son, the Lord Jesus Christ, to us. Thank You for such a wonderful gift! In Jesus' name. Amen.

Day 124 - The Proud Pharisee

A Pharisee was a very religious man in Jesus' day. He studied the Bible, and he was always praying. There was one proud Pharisee who thought he did everything right. Then there was the Publican, a man who knew little about the Bible. He did not pray and knew he did wrong things.

One day, the two went up to the temple to pray. The Pharisee looked at the Publican. Then he said to God, "Thank You I am not like this man. I fast, pray, and give money to You. I am sure this Publican does not do as much as I."

The publican knew he was not always good. So, he asked God to forgive him for the bad things he had done.

Jesus told the people that God accepted the Publican's prayer. He was unhappy with the Pharisee's prayer because he was proud and thought he was better. God hates pride, and He prefers when we are humble, like the Publican.

Which one sounds like you?

Day 125 - Prayer

God, I bless Your holy name for who You are. Help me not to be proud like the Pharisee. Your Word tells us that You hate pride. We also know that it goes before a fall. You also tell us that You will fight against those who are proud. When we are proud, we only think about ourselves and not others. That is not good. Please give me a meek and humble spirit that will not boast and think that I am better than other people. Thank You for the answer. In Jesus' name. Amen.

Day 126 - Too Busy For God

Once a king's son was going to get married. He invited all his family and friends to the wedding. The king prepared a large feast when the day came and waited for his guests to arrive. But many of them did not show up. They gave him all kinds of excuses for why they could not attend. Some had gone to their farms, and another to look at something new he had bought. They were just too busy doing their own thing. The king was very upset. So, he sent his servants into town to invite anyone who wanted to come. Many people came and enjoyed the feast that the others had missed.

Sometimes, we are too busy for God, and we miss the blessings He wants us to have.

What always keeps you busy?

Day 127 - Prayer

Dear God, thank You because You are not too busy for us. May I never be too busy for You, O Lord. Let me find time to talk with You, read Your Word, pray and worship You. Help me put You first in my life. Thank You, wonderful God. In Jesus' name. Amen.

Day 128 – The Ten Lepers

As Jesus was going through a particular village, He met ten lepers. These were people with terrible skin diseases. Because other people could catch it from them, they had to live by themselves. No family or friends could come near them. Imagine how they felt. They cried out to Jesus from afar and begged Him to heal them. Jesus told the ten lepers to go and show themselves to the priest. As they obeyed Him and went, they received their healing. Can you imagine how happy they were? But only one of the ten ran back to Jesus and gave Him thanks.

We must never forget to thank God for the good things He does for us every day.

Do you remember to thank God when you wake up every morning?

Do you thank your parents before you eat or after you have eaten?

Day 129 – Prayer

L et us give thanks to our God, for He is good. Let us praise Him for the good works He has done for all of us. He sends rain on the good and the bad. He gives us life, health, and strength. Let us praise Him for all the blessings He gives us. Let us thank Him for His mercy and forgiveness. Let everyone thank and praise the Lord. Hallelujah! In Jesus' name. Amen.

Day 130 – The Ten Bridesmaids

J esus told a story about a young woman who was getting married. She asked ten of her friends to be her bridesmaids. They got dressed and were waiting to be taken to the wedding. They waited all day until night came. They were tired and fell asleep. Then they heard the bridegroom had arrived in the middle of the night. It was time to get to the wedding. They quickly woke up, put on their clothes, and grabbed their lamps. They needed the light from the lamp to get to the wedding because it was dark. But only five of them had oil in their lamps. The other five did not. So only those who had the oil went off to the wedding. They left the other five behind and they missed the wedding.

That tells us we will miss out on essential things if we are not ready.

You or your parents, who get ready for a church service first?

Have you ever missed a great function because you were not ready in time?

Do you like waiting for people?

Do you go to school late? Why?

Day 131 - Prayer

God, thank You for giving us a Promised Land—Heaven. I want to be ready when You come back to earth to take us there. Let me do everything as Your Word tells me. I want to keep shining for You until You come. Heavenly Father, help me be ready when Jesus comes back for us. I mean this prayer with all my heart. You have always answered me when I ask You for something. Thank You for that. In Jesus' name, I pray. Amen.

Day 132 - Jesus Rides on a Donkey

O n the last week of Jesus' life on earth, He wanted His people, the Jews, to know that He was the King God had promised them long ago. So, He sent His disciples to get a donkey for Him to ride on. He especially wanted to ride on a donkey. You see...; it was already written in the Bible that their King would one day come to them, riding on a donkey. Jesus knew that this was the day for Him to do that. He told His disciples where to find the donkey and that they should tell the owner He needed to use it. The disciples saw the donkey, as Jesus said, and the owner gave it to them. When they came back, they put some of their clothes on the donkey for Jesus to sit on. Then they set off for Jerusalem.

What kind of vehicle does your president, prime minister, king, or ruler use when going to a function?

Does your ruler have a driver and escort personnel?

What example do you think Jesus showed us when He rode on a donkey?

Day 133 - Prayer

Father, thank You because Jesus has shown me an excellent example of being humble. Jesus was so humble that He rode on a donkey. Let me not be proud and boastful or try to show off. I want to be just like Jesus. Lord, I praise Your name because I know You will help me deal with pride. In Jesus' name. Amen.

Day 134 - Jesus Goes to Jerusalem

J esus rode on a donkey to Jerusalem. His disciples followed Him. As He got near the city, the people came out to meet Him. Some remembered that the Bible said their King would come to them riding on a donkey. They believed Jesus was from the family of King David.

So, they started shouting, "Hosanna to the Son of David! Blessed is He who comes in the name of the Lord!"

The disciples were also shouting praises to God for all the miracles and good things Jesus had been doing. People waved palm branches and spread them on the ground with their garments for the donkey to walk on, creating a lot of noise. They welcomed Jesus like a king. Oh, of course, Jesus is the King of Kings.

If Jesus showed up in your town, what would you do? And did the leaders of the Jews crown Jesus as a king?

Day 135 - Prayer

F ather God, I worship Your name because of the gift of Your Son to us. I welcome Your Son, Jesus Christ, as King into my heart. He is a wonderful, kind, and loving King. I bow down and worship Him today for what He did for us all. Please help me tell others about Him so that they will come and worship Him. Thank You, Jesus, for always being willing to enter the heart of anyone that wants You in their life. In Jesus' name. Amen.

Day 136 - Jesus and the Leaders of the Jews

W hen Jesus, His disciples, and the people came into the city, everyone wondered what was happening. Why were the people so excited, crowding around Jesus and shouting, "Hosanna to the Son of David!' Blessed is He who comes in the name of the Lord!' Hosanna in the highest!" (Mathew 21:9).

"Who is this man?" the leaders asked the people because they did not believe Jesus was anyone special.

The people said, "Jesus, the prophet from Nazareth."

Some leaders told Jesus to tell His followers to be quiet and stop saying all those things about Him. But Jesus told them, "If the people did not speak, then the rocks would cry out."

That was Jesus' way of telling them that what the people were saying about Him was true. But the leaders did not want to believe it. For most of the week, Jesus taught the people in the temple in Jerusalem. But the leaders were very upset and kept thinking of a way to get rid of Him.

How would you feel if you tell someone who you are and the person does not believe thinking you are lying?

Since not everybody would believe what you say, what strategies do you need to learn to deal with such situations?

Day 137 - Prayer

F ather, I worship You for being so generous in sending Your Son to save us. I know Jesus is unique. He is Your only Son, who came down from Heaven to save us from our sins, and He did it out of His great love for us. Thank You for sending Jesus. Jesus, thank You for coming to save us. In Jesus' name. Amen.

Day 138 - Martha and Mary

Jesus had some friends in Bethany. They were Martha, Mary, and their brother, Lazarus. He stayed at their house sometimes when He came to Jerusalem. Martha loved to cook, and whenever Jesus came, she busied herself in the kitchen. On one of His visits, she was very busy getting a meal ready. She was in the kitchen, but her sister, Mary, was sitting at Jesus' feet, listening to what He was saying. Martha got upset because Mary was not helping her. She went and complained to Jesus. Then Jesus told her that Mary had chosen to listen to Him, which was the better thing to do. She, Martha, was spending too much time in the kitchen. He told her she needed to spend more time with Him than cooking.

Just like Mary, we all need to spend more time with Jesus.

Name some ways we can spend time with Jesus.

What do you do with your parents when they spend time with you?

Day 139 - Prayer

God, thank You for putting Your Word in written form so we can use it to correct one another, as Jesus corrected Martha. Martha, Mary's sister, was too busy to listen to Jesus. That happens to me, too. I get busy with so many things that I do not have enough time to read my Bible and pray. Please help me know that talking and listening to You is the most crucial thing in my day. Please help me make more time to do this. Thank You, Lord, for everyone You are using to point me in the right direction. In Jesus' name. I pray. Amen.

Day 140 - Lazarus Gets Sick

One day, Lazarus, Jesus' friend, got sick. Jesus was far away, so Mary and Martha sent messengers to tell him about Lazarus. Mary and Martha were very upset and wondered why Jesus was not coming so He could heal their brother. They knew He could make Lazarus better. They waited and waited, but Jesus did not come. And so, their brother, Lazarus, died. Jesus reached their house four days after they had buried Lazarus. Mary and Martha wept and told Him their brother would not have died if He had come sooner.

Jesus told them not to worry, just to believe in Him, and they would see their brother again. They did not know how this would help now that they had buried their brother for four days. Then Jesus asked them to take Him to where they buried Lazarus.

What was Jesus going to do there?

Day 141 - Jesus Calls Lazarus From the Tomb

Mary and Martha wondered what Jesus was going to do at the tomb of Lazarus, their brother. He was already dead and buried for four days. But they obeyed Jesus and took Him to the grave. When Jesus arrived there, He, too, cried because Lazarus was His friend. They buried Lazarus in a cave with a big stone covering its mouth, and Jesus told them to take away the stone. They wondered if Jesus knew what He was doing, but they did as He asked, regardless.

Then Jesus prayed and said in a loud voice, "Lazarus, come forth!"

Everyone waited to see what would happen.

Have you ever spoken to anything that cannot reply to you before?

What did you speak to?

Day 142 - Prayer

T hank You, God, for Your assurance of hope for every-one that believes in Your Son, Jesus Christ. Jesus says He will bring us back to life one day, even if we die now. That is very hard to understand, but I believe it is true. Lord, I can't wait to see that wonderful day. Thank You for it.

Father God, thank You because You can do all things. Help me accept that You may not answer our prayers right away. Please help me trust that You know what is best for me. I bless Your name for doing everything for my good. In Jesus' name. Amen.

Day 143 - Lazarus Comes Alive Again

M ary, Martha, Jesus' disciples, and other people waited to see what would happen. Jesus had gone to Lazarus' tomb and called for him to come out of it. Nobody on earth had ever done anything like this before. They were surprised to see Lazarus sit up in the tomb as they waited, and he was still wrapped up in the pieces of cloth they had buried him in.

Jesus said, "Lose him and let him go!"

Some braver persons, who were not trembling in fear and awe, ran towards Lazarus and unwrapped him. He was happy to be alive again, and so were his two sisters.

Everyone could not stop talking about the incredible power that Jesus had. As the Son of God, He can bring people back from the dead.

That is awesome!

Jesus had that great power, and He gave it to you, too, so you can use it whenever you need to. Now you can speak to pain to get out of your body, and you can speak smartness, grace, etc., into your life. Please speak nothing negative concerning you or other people.

What are you going to speak to today?

Day 144 - Prayer

God, thank You for Your power of resurrection. It was an amazing miracle for Jesus to bring back Lazarus from the dead. That tells me He is Your beloved Son, who can do anything. I know we will all die someday, but because of what He said and did when raising Lazarus, I know that one day, He will bring all God's children back to live with Him forever. I can hardly wait for that lovely day to come. Even so, hurry, and come back, Lord Jesus. Thank You again for that great day. In Jesus' name. Amen.

Day 145 - The Ten Talents

This is a story Jesus told of a rich man who had many servants. The rich man was going away on a long trip. So, he called his servants together. He gave them some money, called talents, to look after while he was away. He gave one ten, the other five, and one to the third person. He told them to use the money he had given them wisely to make more money for him.

They call that investing so that the money you have will become more. After being away for a very long time, the master came back. He called his three servants to see what they had done with his money.

What do you think they all did with the money he gave them?

Day 146 - Prayer

G od, thank you for being so generous to me. I want to know what You have given me to use for You until Jesus comes back. I can do some things very well like dance, sing, play a sport, learn something and much more. Please, Lord, help me understand what You want me to do. Thank You for giving me so many talents. In Jesus' name. Amen.

Day 147 - The Wise Servants and the Foolish One

T he master called his servants to ask them about the money he had given them to use for him while he was away. The first servant used his ten talents and earned ten more. He now had twenty talents to give his master. The master was very pleased, and he made him ruler over ten cities. The other servant made five extra talents on his master's money. He had ten talents to give to his master. Again, the master praised him and asked him to rule over five cities. Then came the last servant, who had been given one talent. He gave back the one talent to his master. He told him he was afraid to do anything with it, so he had hidden it. The master was very upset with him for not doing anything with the money. So, he took it from him and gave it to the servant who had earned ten talents.

Jesus wanted his hearers to know that we must always use the talents God gives us, or we will lose them.

What would you use it for if you were given money to invest?

Day 148 - Prayer

God, I praise You because You created every one of us, each filled with different talents. You promise to give us prizes for the work we do for You while we live on earth. You have given all of us talents to use for You. Help me find my talent and use it well so that when You come back, You will say to me, "Well done!" Thank You for You are the Great Giver. In Jesus' name. Amen.

Day 149 - To Obey or Not to Obey

A certain man had two sons.

One day, he said to one of them, "Go and work on the farm today."

The son said, "Yes," but he did not go.

He said to his other son, "Go work on the farm today."

He said, "No."

But later, the one that said no changed his mind and went while the other son that said yes did not go. Jesus asked the people to tell Him which of the two sons was the obedient one. Was it the one who said he would go and did not? Or was it the one who said he would not go but, in the end, went?

I think you know which one it is—the second one. It is better to say no, and then do it than to say you're going to do it and don't. God wants us always to keep our promises.

Have you behaved like these two sons before?

When you said yes, why did you not keep to your promise?

When you said no, what changed your mind?

Day 150 - Prayer

Lord, thank You for promising to send Your son Jesus back to earth for all who believe. Help me keep my promise and do whatever You tell me to do. Let me not be too ready to say yes and then don't. Thank You for showing us several times that You will always keep Your promises to us, no matter what. In Jesus' name. Amen.

Day 151 - Dorcas, the Kind Woman

There was a woman named Dorcas living in Joppa. She heard the good news about Jesus Christ and became a Christian. Dorcas looked around her for something she could do to help others. She saw that many poor people did not have clothes. So, she made clothes for them. One day, she became sick and died. The people were crying, saying, "Dorcas was so good to us, and now she is gone. Who is going to sew clothes for us and help us?" Then they heard that Peter was preaching in a town nearby.

Quickly, they sent for him. They told him all about Dorcas' good works, and now she was dead. Peter went into the room, prayed to God, and told Dorcas to come back alive. God answered Peter's prayer, and the dead Dorcas came back to life. That is how we know Jesus has given His miracle-working power to His disciples.

Have you ever prayed for someone sick before? Oh..., don't say you are too little because God uses the rich, poor, elder, and little children.

Day 152 - Prayer

My faithful Father, thank You for the gift of feeling that You have given to us. Your Word tells us we should be kind to each other. I get a nice feeling when people are kind to me. Teach me how to be kind and help others. Help me follow Your example of kindness. Thank You, dear Lord. In Jesus' name. Amen.

Day 153 – Saul, the Enemy of Christians

S aul did not like the Christians at all. He didn't believe Jesus was God's Son. Because of this, after Jesus went back to Heaven, Saul tried to stop His disciples from telling people about Him. The priests in charge of Jerusalem's temple also thought the same way. So, Saul took letters from them to hunt down the Christians. When he found them, he was to bring them to Jerusalem to be tried and punished for believing in Jesus. You can imagine that every Christian was afraid of Saul and kept running away from him. That continued until something strange happened to Saul.

What would you do if someone asked you to stop talking about Jesus?

Day 154 - Prayer

God, thank You because You know everything about everyone. Sometimes people are unkind to me because I say I am a Christian, and they laugh at me and tease me. Help me be brave and not stop believing in You because of what they do or say. And for the unkind people who do not believe in You worldwide, please help Your children talk to them about You. Thank You for the answered prayers. In Jesus' name. Amen.

Day 155 - Paul Falls off His Horse

S aul started going to Damascus so he could hunt down the believers of Jesus Christ, and he would take them back to Jerusalem to be punished by the High Priest. Neither he nor the priests believed that Jesus Christ was the Son of God and the Savior of the World. They did not want Jesus' disciples telling this to other people.

Saul was riding on his horse with many soldiers. Suddenly, a light, brighter than the sun, appeared in the sky. It frightened Saul's horse, and he fell off. Then Saul heard a voice calling his name.

"Saul, Saul, why are you persecuting me?"

Immediately, Saul knew it was Jesus talking to him, and so he said, "Who are You, Lord?"

The voice said, "I am Jesus, who you are trying to hurt."

Saul knew what this meant. When you try to hurt God's people, it is like you are hurting God. We must never forget this.

What happened next?

Day 156 - Prayer

Dear God, I can't stop thanking You for Your Son, Jesus; who knows when someone is hurt. Let me remember that when I am hurting, You are there with me. It is like You, God, are hurting, too, because You live in my heart. Let me remember this and pray to You no matter how I feel. I praise You, O God, for always being with me. In Jesus' name. Amen.

Day 157 - Saul Becomes Blind

S aul and some soldiers were traveling to Damascus to find and lock up Christians. But as he was on the way, a bright light from Heaven shone around him, and he fell off his horse. Then he heard the voice of Jesus talking to him. Jesus told Saul to go into the city, and someone would come and tell him what to do. After hearing this and getting up from the ground, Saul realized he was blind. He could not see. The bright light from Heaven had hurt his eyes. Someone had to lead him around. They took him to a house in the city, and they left him there.

What was going to happen to Saul now?

Day 158 - Ananias Told to Visit Saul

L iving in the city of Damascus was a man named Ananias. As a follower of Jesus Christ, he belonged to the group of people Saul was trying to lock up. One day, he was praying, and God spoke to him. He told him to go and visit Saul, who was staying in a particular house in Damascus. Ananias was not sure he had heard God right. He, a Christian whom Saul was trying to kill, was to visit Saul? He asked God about this, and God said yes, this was the man He was sending him to see.

Ananias was very afraid, but he had to obey God. God told him that Saul was blind, and that he should go and pray for him so he could see again. That was strange, but Ananias always did what God told him to do. So, he left his house and went to find Saul.

If you were Ananias, would you do this?

How would you feel and why?

Day 159 - Prayer

Father in Heaven, thank You for You are a good God. Please make me an obedient servant who will always do what You tell me. When I am afraid to obey You, give me the courage to go, knowing that You are with me. Make me brave enough to tell my friends and others about You. Thank You, Lord, for giving me a heart that obeys Your Word. In Jesus' name. Amen.

Day 160 - Saul Waits on God

With a trembling heart, Ananias made his way through the streets of Damascus. He would see a man known for hunting down Christians like him. But God said he should go, so he was on his way.

In the meantime, Saul was in the house of Judas, wondering what was going to happen to him. It has now been three days since he fell off his horse and went blind. Since then, he had had nothing to eat or drink. He had also heard the voice of Jesus telling him to go into the city and wait for a man to come to him. Through this man, he would get back his sight. All this was very weird, but there was nothing Saul could do but wait.

Sometimes, we, too, have to learn to wait for what God has promised us.

If you were Saul, how would you feel now?

Day 161 - Prayer

Dear God, thank You because You are always with me. Lord, even when something terrible happens to me, You are there with me. Thank You for this and let me learn to pray and wait on You to help me because I know You always will. Thank You for that. In Jesus' name. Amen.

Day 162 - Saul can See Again

O bedient Ananias went to the house of Judas and found Saul. The two of them were not sure exactly what was going on, but God had spoken to them. So, Ananias prayed for Saul, just as God told him to do. Immediately, Saul's eyes opened, and he could see again.

That was not all. Saul changed his heart about Jesus while waiting for Ananias to come. When Ananias finished praying for Saul, Saul asked to be baptized. That meant he now believed that Jesus Christ was the Son of God and the world's Savior. That was wonderful, good news.

He no longer wanted to chase and capture Christians, and he was now one of them. Later, Saul changed his name to Paul and wrote many of the books in the New Testament. God certainly knows how to help us believe in Him.

Do you believe that Jesus Christ is the Son of God?

Do you also want to become a follower of Jesus, like Ananias and Paul?

Day 163 - Prayer

Dear Father, thank You for Your loving-kindness. I always want to be with Your Son, Jesus, because He is kind, good, and loving. He promised to get a place ready for me so that I could live with Him one day, and I can't wait for that to happen. Thank You, my Father, for loving me this much. In Jesus' name. Amen.

Day 164 – Jesus Blesses the Children

J esus was going all over Israel, preaching and teaching. Huge crowds of men, women, and children followed Him. Some wanted to hear what He was teaching. Others wanted Him to heal their sicknesses, and some only wanted to see Him.

One day, some women wanted Him to bless their children. These women and their children pushed their way to the front of the crowd, but the disciples would have none of it. They began chasing away the women and their children. When Jesus saw this, He stopped them. He asked the women to bring their children to Him. He took the children up in His arms and blessed all of them. The mothers and children were very happy. Jesus, the Son of God, had blessed them. Jesus wants all children to know that He loves them and wants to bless them. Receive His blessings today!

Do you know Jesus wants you to be with Him all the time?

Do you know He knows your name and the number of the hair on your head?

Day 165 - Prayer

Dear God, thank You for Your only Son, Jesus Christ. I believe that Jesus Christ is Your Son, and that He came into the world as a baby, just like me. He is no longer a baby. He is my Savior, and He wants to bless me. I receive His blessing today. I also receive His gift of life to me, and I receive Him into my heart. Thank You, because even if I am a child, He is with me. In Jesus' name. Amen.

Conclusion

Wow! We made it! I thank you for finishing this book with me. It was a wonder going through all the stories and prayers. I believe you have learned a lot. Keep it up! Would you please consider some of my other books so that we can continue this journey together? I can't do this without you, you know?

Please consider ordering one if you did not start with our Old Testament Amazing Moments storybook. It has 200 days of either a story or a prayer, and it also has a coloring book to go with it.

This book is the very first in a series for children. The next will be for children eight years and older, and it has stories and prayers for the same day, meaning with that book, you will be praying every day. I encourage you to purchase the other one. Check our Amazon store, and you will find ways I can help you in your walk with God.

I would love to see many other children taught God's truths in their homes. If I was valuable to you in that way, please leave an honest review on Amazon, and other parents will be encouraged to teach their children about God–with my help.

God bless you and yours! In Jesus' name. Amen!

Only One Life!

Resources

Youversion. (1996). [Computer software]. Life Church. https://www.youversion.com/the-bible-app/

Also By Only One Life

Biblical Bedtime Stories for Kids: Old Testament Amazing Moments Pointing Your Children to God, Ages 4 – 8.

Biblical Bedtime Stories for Kids: 113 Old Testament Amazing Moments Pointing Your Children to God Coloring Book, Ages 4 – 8.

Biblical Questions and Answers for Smart Kids: Quizzes Focused on the Book of Genesis to Help Your Children Grow and Learn about God – Who He is, His Love, and His Relationship with Humanity.

Biblical Characters for Kids: Adventures of the Patriarchs God Wants Your Children to Know, Ages 7-12.

About Author

"Only One Life" writes with a heart to help children know and love God from an early age. Through simple stories and biblical truths, their books give parents and teachers tools to guide children toward faith in Jesus and a strong foundation that will last a lifetime. Each story is written to spark imagination, open conversation, and lead young readers closer to the God who loves them.

Learn, grow, and love God together...